hello, dear one...

Katrina Warme

sweeterpoetry
volume one

hello, dear one… by Katrina Warme

sweeterpoetry, volume one

www.hellodearone.tumblr.com

Copyright © 2016 Katrina Warme.

All rights reserved. This book or any portion thereof may not be reproduced or used in any manner whatsoever without the express written permission of the author except for the use of brief quotations in a book review. For permissions contact: sweeterchord@icloud.com

First Printing, 2016

ISBN: 1514875985
ISBN-13: 978-1514875988

All poems, prose, and photographs (on the cover and within) are the original work and intellectual property of Katrina Warme, except the photo on p.99, donated by Ann Helen Myrmo. Used with permission.

instagram and twitter: @sweeterchord

photography: www.katrinadphotography.com

To the God who is worthy of all
To the family that loves me completely
To the friends that support me stubbornly
To the encouragers that keep me dreaming
To the ones that will read these words

Thank you.

This is for you.

Hello, dear one

—Katrina
Warn

Author's Note:

I wrestled for a long time with how to compile this book: which poems to include, what story I wanted to tell, how many sections it might have, and whether I should even share it at all. But then I remembered that's not how life works. Life is not divided into clear-cut sections for ease of organization or clarity. Life is. It flows, gets stuck, and we must fight our way through.

So this is that journey: The journey of growing from a trembling hummingbird into a brave phoenix, of learning who you are and how to stand again, of finally trusting the God who made you and calls you His own.

This is hope, for you.

I hope these words resonate with you. I hope that you are able to have a moment where something clicks and you begin to see yourself anew - through a clearer lens this time - and you begin to stop fearing so much.

That's what I want for you. You are why I write. And in these pages are wrought my deepest prayers: that we would know that we matter. And that we are loved.

You are loved, dear one.

Welcome to the journey.

    - *Katrina*

P.S. There's still room for you to write your own.

CONTENTS

Introduction	i
For when you feel (alone)	1
For when you learn to fly (together)	27
For when you fall (again)	63
For when you soar	101
Index	131
For you	139

INTRODUCTION

hello, dear one...

Introduction

The following poem is the best "about the author" I can offer.

This is my struggle, tears, aches, and joy as I moved from feeling alone to learning how to fly - then falling, completely, before I finally began to soar.

But in reality, this is not about me. It is Christ. His redemption, God's voice, the comfort and challenge of a Father who loves. He is why the phoenix flies.

This is meant to be a spoken word piece. Please take the time to hear it as such.

Find the video here: tinyurl.com/littlestphoenix

• [The Littlest Phoenix] •

I have just one thing to say to you. And I'm not really sure I'm going to get another chance. So please listen.

I need you to move.

I need you to pick yourself up off of this ground that you've started to call home and remember who you are.

And I need to you to realize that in order for something lost to be found, it has to be missing in the first place - and you never were - even when you felt most like it. You were here. And I saw you. I saw you scratch your name into the dirt, just testing how it felt to BE for once in your life - but softly, so as to brush it away as someone comes by to read it – **but you're forgetting that it's tattooed into your skin so deeply that even lasers cannot remove you from your own bones.**

Move.

Yes, you! You with the "can you even see me?" nametag, stuck slantwise on someone else's chest because no matter how many times you told me you'd try to find the right person you keep trying to be this one – and I miss you.

Move.

Let this song hold you, even if you don't know what's playing. Even if the world cannot hear the melody that's coursing through your colorful veins like the lifeblood of who you are becoming. They will stare. They will tell you that you are strange and that you do not belong in their world, but hold fast.

And don't you dare hold still.

Someday, someone will hear the same thing and they will plug themselves into the lifeblood you cling to, and they will say, "hello." They will recognize that the pushing and pulling of your soul upon theirs is infinitely more valuable than a "how are you," and more than enough to acquaint you.

And they will tell you that your song is beautiful.

I just wonder if you're going to believe it.

Move.

Encased in something harder than yourself, struggling to get comfortable in this plaster that no longer fits your song. "It's safe." But for how long? The bruises on my elbows are beginning to add their harmony to the chorus of my angles and I'm just not sure how much more of this I can take. You see, I don't know what's outside, but it has to be better than this inside. Better than the darkness that keeps pushing inward even as I grow outward and as much as I try to hold back, to keep fitting, the sun is a magnet to my soul and I will not suffocate again.

Move.

The worst is over, right? Wrong. Now you fall. Plummet. Step off of that ledge into the abyss and find your wings on the way down…

NOBODY TOLD ME IT WOULD TAKE THIS LONG TO FLY!

Move.

If this pain is thunder then you are the lightning that I stay up late every night to watch make its way across this marbled sky.

Move.

I saw them hurt you. I saw them tear you apart feather by feather until you forgot what it felt like to fly.

And then, you got up, opened your heart wider than before, and soared.

hello, dear one...

FOR WHEN YOU FEEL (ALONE)

hello, dear one…

• [**The Letters She Wrote Were To Herself**] •

These words are imperfect. They are raw. They are my heart's clamor and the ways that God has spoken to me. But they aren't enough. So look to His Word. Look to the beauty of the fact that He thinks you're precious and valuable enough to pay for you with His Son. Look at the beauty in His grace toward you as He holds you while you grow. And look in awe at the way He flows through you even as you are cracking and feeling broken. You shine, dear one. You are precious. And yes, on your own, you will never be enough.

But that's the point.

You are enough because He is in you. And since that will never change, neither will this:

You are enough.

• [The One That Remains] •

There's so much I want to tell you. I even made a list.

I made a list of three, seventeen, four hundred…and then just one:

I only stand because He stood again.

That's all that matters. That's all that will last.

But if you stay, someday I'll tell you the rest.

• [The Place Where Solitude is Born] •

"I think sometimes you don't see yourself."

Maybe more than sometimes, dear one. I've defined deflection as humility and now I no longer know how to believe you.

• [The Struggle Of Sunset] •

It is the curse of the poet, therefore, that to understand she must understand herself; but for others to understand, she must deny the depths of the burden within.

(At least that's what they say.)

I'm sick of "what they say."

• [The Unkempt Souls] •

I'm not sure you realize how much effort this takes. To breathe.

• [The Marvelous Ones] •

Sometimes, often, everyday, the most prodigious thing you can do is stay standing. And refuse to be any less than who you are.

• [The Resisting Is Like Chemo Sometimes] •

Maybe it's hard sometimes to hear whether my words are about myself or someone else. Maybe they're even about you, dear ones. (They are.)

But lately I've realized the truth of what I said long ago: that my poetry is the language of my soul. It is my heart's desperate plea when my brain doesn't get it and is stuck behind lies.

I stopped writing, you see, because I got stuck. Stuck again in those thick tendrils of doubt I thought I left behind long ago. Not anymore.

So here's one. And this is for me,

I am stronger than the voices in my head.

And Your voice is louder.

• [The Lies That Fog The Mirror] •

It's not that they changed you. You just believed them for so long that now you can't see yourself anymore, here, still just as beautiful, even though you're broken - even though you're healing.

(I see you. I'm still here.)

• [The Subtext] •

Sometimes, I think, when we say, "how are you?" we're really just asking, "you see me too, right?"

• [The Shadows Have A Voice] •

"Write this down," he said.

"And keep going even when you run out of ink.

You are enough."

hello, dear one...

• [The Pebbles In My Pockets] •

When words aren't enough. When photos fade into sepia. When ink bleeds and pens refuse to move.

These will be my memories. And they will someday add up to a weight that demands to be noticed.

And I will carry them.

Until I finally remember who I am.

• [The Dream Quilt] •

...There's a girl, in the corner, embodying all the heaviness of the word sigh as she tries for the fifty-fourth time (just today) to pick herself up off this floor and join the rest of the passing shadows that have somehow taught themselves to survive breathing something less than oxygen. Inhale. Exhaustion.

"I'm not okay today." she says, part excuse, part cry. A quiet comment (Laced with desperation) - as monotone as greyscale but tumultuous as an EKG but at least it reminds her that her heart is still beating...

|| Full poem on soundcloud.com/sweeterchord ||

• [The Walkway Doesn't End Here] •

Look, I know that you're feeling alone. I know that it's dark outside and there are no stars and maybe the wolves are howling too, and you can't imagine how you'll get through the night.

But can I tell you something?

You can't see the stars when your eyes are closed. The howling is nothing more than the echo of waves distorted by your hurts. And it's daytime here, outside of your shell.

And hope is the sun.

• [The Reflections Lie] •

Sometimes I don't think you realize that you're living in a room of fun house mirrors and everything tells you the opposite. And every moment you forget this is another step toward forgetting forever.

So what will you tell yourself today, to remember?

May I make a suggestion?

Tell yourself that you are beautiful.

And I'll tell you that you are strong.

• [The One You Skipped] •

If you're reading this and I'm no longer here, I hope you knew.

But if you still don't, there's a tape hidden under the back staircase of the old house with one track on repeat.

I told you I'd keep saying this until you believed me. Even if I have no words left.

• [The Bruises On Our Knuckles] •

Every day, talented people are told "you can't."

Every day, passionate people are told "that's not enough."

And every day, they turn to these voices and say "no." They keep going, so that someday, soon, you won't have to face these anymore.

• [The Snowflake Mold Broke Today] •

How much easier it is to believe that each is unique than that we are, even though they're gone in a moment and I don't need a microscope to see you.

(I still like your edges.)

• [The Dichotomies In My Head] •

This is. And isn't. And is. And I really have no way to explain to you how it's all held together but, somehow, sometimes, you just have to believe because otherwise everything you think you know turns to ash and the wind takes it.

There it goes. And that's my point.

Because you're still here.

Aren't you?

• [The Dawn In Me] •

Did you know that today and tomorrow together topple the torridity of yesterday?

(Translation:

It's okay to let go.)

Hear that. Someday. Please?

• [The Ink Doesn't Have To Go On Paper] •

Yeah yeah, I've heard the excuses. The lines of false humility that create the masks we hide behind. "Theirs is more important. I don't have a story. No no, I'll go next."

Next is now, dear ones. You matter.

For when you feel (alone)

• [The Day You Screened Darkness' Call] •

"I feel for you"

But I am.

Walking around with your lungs inside of me, trembling and straining against the confines of this cage that they've said will protect you (but feels more like a cave than a home), trying to make your way toward a beat that seems steadier than your own.

"You are safe here."

I promise.

hello, dear one...

• [The Clifftop Is A Cave] •

Can I tell you a secret?

It's okay to be lost.

It's okay to teeter on tiptoes -

about to fall -

leaning on the wind

ballerina hands flying

and eyes shut

tightly.

It's okay.

As long as you stay.

Here.

With me.

And let me catch you

if you fall.

(Please catch me)

(when I fall.)

For when you feel (alone)

• [The Stranger Tides] •

"You are the sunset," he says, "that the ocean never grows tired of embracing, day after day (after day) - and you know that here, you are home. You are loved."

But some days, I feel like sand-soaked jeans and rock-bruised toes

and it's just

so hard

to remember.

"Please try."

• [The End Of Tomorrow] •

Is never more severe than the end of yesterday, as long as you realize that you're now closer to who you want to be and today is still important.

(Be here.)

It's not over yet.

• [The Light That Knows You Better Than The Dark Places] •

Somewhere inside, where you don't want to admit you still fear, there's a song sitting, waiting - no. Clamoring, fighting, fending off the voices until you hear it scream your name and realize that you are heard, here.

• [The Tree Swings] •

Any way the wind takes it, or so they say, but not when we add our own weight - reminding these branches that they too are real and we, we are in this together.

(Don't fall.)

• [The Sunrises You Sleep Through] •

We've missed too many moments, over here, looking down at our toes, hoping for something to change.

• [The Faceless Mirror] •

In a world where we walk by and pretend to not notice one another, how can we be surprised to find that we are not often seen?

• [The Bravery Of Hearing] •

We are lost here within ourselves, I think. Afraid to be who we were. Scared to be who we are becoming. Unable to be who we are - extra tree limbs in clifftop fog waiting for the sun to find us again but too afraid to burn.

I forget, sometimes, that my favorite sound is rain through those mist-wrapped fingers. Not because I'm waiting for your tears - I'm just here, if you'll let me be.

• [The Sound The Tree Made When It Fell In The Middle Of The Woods] •

I thought you said it didn't matter.

• [The Other Ninety-Percent Feels Too] •

We are frozen. We are moving. We are the ice that people fear but that forces them to heal, reminding them that numbness is intended to make us feel again, not remove our nerves like an appendectomy of the feeling we think no longer necessary. (But it is.)

We are stuck. We are fighting. We are bound merely by our own fear but never forgetting the life bubbling up inside of us and pushing us to go. To feel. To be so much more than this fear says we can be - because even this world is not enough weight to keep our tomb closed. (Keep pushing.)

We are afraid. We are alive. We are shaking so much that we can't even stand, but we will shake until the chains fall off, if that's what it takes. Because fear cannot hold us. Not anymore. Not like this.

"Will you be there with me?"

Not always. But today I will be. And I will stay.

• [The Misunderstanding Effect] •

I just want you to know that sunsets through scratched train windows are still just as beautiful and I think you're forgetting that your mirror is a liar.

• [The Truth About Idioms] •

Look, it's not that today's seed is tomorrow's orchard. It's that today's seed is next month's sapling and you may very well spend the rest of your life craving apple juice, but just know that I'm waiting for it too. With you.

hello, dear one...

• [The Longest Tunnel]•

Loving is scary.

You depend and you give and life will never be the same again but one of these days, tomorrow or 2070, one of you is going to be gone (and that scares me sometimes) but, I have to tell you, if you let it, the fear of the inevitable will leave you lonelier than any one person ever should be (and you can't hold your breath, like this, forever.)

• [The Remnants Of Sunset] •

I tried, all day long, to help you see (what I see) until all I had left to give was to fall, slowly, (too fast); stretching out my colors (for you) so that maybe (hopefully) they'd be enough (to remind you.)

But I'll be back, tomorrow, to bleed for you again, if that's what it takes.

(And the next day) until you, finally, hear (that you're worth it.)

• [The Promise "Someday" Cannot Break] •

I don't care if they've forgotten how to listen (or even how to love). You have never been anything less than loved and your words still matter, here.

For when you feel (alone)

• [The Stroller's Red Umbrella] •

I will shade you from the sun, dear one, until you're ready to walk alone. Until you're ready to not be afraid anymore.

I just hope, someday, you'll choose to stop hiding.

(The rain feels good too.)

(I promise.)

• [The World Is A Bully Sometimes] •

If you're the kid hiding behind the park bench, just so the other kids won't take your popsicle, there's a spot here, next to me, and you can stay as long as you'd like.

• [**The World Is Our Noise-Canceling Headphones**] •

When He says, "I love you," we (too often) hear:

"I love you five years from now when you've gotten your act together. (Why are you taking so long?),"

when, instead, He is saying, "I love you now and in two seconds and in five years (and in every moment that time has existed even when you did not) and I just want you to take your hands off your own ears and hear Me."

("I love you.")

• [**The Three-Year-Old Can't Fall Asleep Yet**] •

Today, I will hold your hands as you weep your doubt and un-belonging. (Where does a child learn the world hate?)

Today, I will sing until your shaking steadies, slowly. (When do we stop remembering how to breathe?)

Today, I will stay - here - with every decibel my soul can muster - that you may know you are loved. You are loved. You are loved. (What will it take for you to hear again?)

For when you feel (alone)

• [**The Things It's Okay To Say Today**] •

"I'm not okay."

You will be.

"I'm stuck."

Not for long.

"I don't know."

I'm here.

"Please stay."

• [The Test Said I Wasn't An Empathizer] •

I cried for strangers today.

We haven't met.

I don't even know their names, their faces, or whether they like cream or sugar with their coffee.

I don't know your struggles, your loves, your tears, or your pain.

But I see you.

I see the twitching way you rub your thumb against the nail on your ring finger, trying to stop the urge to rip at your own skin (I just. have. to feel. something). I see the way you tense when someone brushes against the back of your chair, muttering reassurances to yourself that you're okay (this isn't the same). I see your clenched jaw, your haze-hidden eyes, and your too-quick laughter (did they notice?). I see behind that smile.

I don't know you.

We haven't met.

I cried for you.

• [The Same Bird] •

"I can't do this anymore."

Yes you can.

"I feel too much."

You feel just as much as you ever have.

"It's different."

The only difference between this and all the moments that came before is that there are no walls to keep you from hearing the fear that gnaws on each and every one of your nerves until you can no longer sense your own movement.

"I'm stuck."

No, you're raw.

But here you can be something more than alone.

hello, dear one...

FOR WHEN YOU LEARN TO FLY
(TOGETHER)

hello, dear one...

• [The Heart Is Precious. (Don't Forget)] •

You will learn to fly.

You will learn that it's easier to breathe up here than it ever was on the ground and your wings, they are tougher than Icarus'. They were built to withstand this heat and the sun cannot destroy you. You were made for this.

And then you will be unafraid to soar.

• [The Instruction Manual Is Missing (All Its) Pages] •

"But then how do we find out the reason why someone is in our lives?"

We live.

• [The Newness] •

I am waiting, waiting (waiting)

I am already whole.

I am holding hopes together

with the weight of my soul.

I was never just a cloud

but a wandering instead.

I find my home on clifftops

where the climbing soul hath fled,

to escape the wishful words

of a heart that never knew

it could birth a new beginning

when it learned to fly with you.

• [The Breath In The Fog] •

You remind me of what it is to be so alive that everything around me screams my existence. To be. To breathe. And to remember that the smallest movement of organs unseen is enough to keep me moving.

For when you learn to fly (together)

• [The Resistance] •

I didn't wear my heart on my sleeve, but its heaviness wore holes in all my pockets.

It seemed like a good idea at the time, hiding everything away. But I couldn't do so for long.

The weight would become too much to bear and my heart would fall and sometimes I would trip over it.

I would trip over my own heart, grinding doubt into the cracks where dreams had leaked out and stained the road red.

No more.

No longer shall I hide my heart away. I will hold my dreams in trembling hands; that nobody may trod on them again.

• [The Grammatically Correct Way To Be Crazy] •

(This is my mind sometimes.)

I am only as "stuck" as I allow myself to me and my words are not limited to the moments when they make sense.

(I can no sooner explain it to you than I can to myself.)

I am a cloud. I am a painting behind the glass. I am the raindrops that survive the wind. I am a canvas with a stubbornness of my own. I am the puddles that reflect sunset.

(I am none of these things.)

I am more than these things.

• [The Difference Today] •

I am shaking. My hands have forgotten to move. I am spinning. (No I'm not.)

They stop when you hold them, I guess that's how I know. I don't need you. I'm okay here. This is normal.

But when you hold me, I remember that I already was whole. I am real. I belong here, in this moment, and I can stay. Here. With you.

Okay.

For when you learn to fly (together)

• [The Game Gravity Plays] •

No matter where I am, this earth mocks me. It mocks me with hopelessness like the fraying string of a kite, bitterness like the tree's sharp embrace, and pain like the brokenness felt with every inch of the fall.

I've been wandering this land too long. Stuck. To the point where, even up here, floating, the sky feels too far away. I feel no closer to those stars nor to the dreams I ascribe to them.

They are out of my reach.

But someday, I will fly.

(Today.)

• [The Heart Grew Three Sizes Today] •

And in that instant, my capacity to love was a rocket to Saturn; drawn by the significance behind its rings and the fact that we have never been farther from lonely than we are in this moment.

"Why does this matter so much?"

If I have to explain, you haven't been there yet. It'll happen; when you realize someone is so much dearer to you than you could have imagined and, now, here, you understand the significance of becoming part of a new family; when you realize you'd give your own breath for the life of someone you'd never before known.

"If this is the collateral of your love, I'm not sure my heart can handle my own yet."

Seeds, dear one, grow in time.

• [The Dictionary Is Incomplete] •

"I love you yesterday, today, and tomorrow," they promise with lying lips that do not understand that I will not be this same me. For I am a phoenix burning off all of my feathers so that I may start again and you are shedding skin just to show that you existed somewhere deeper, but tomorrow you will not know me anymore.

For when you learn to fly (together)

• [The Repurposed Anchors] •

Do you know what it is to be here? Simultaneously wrapped up in your own fears and dreams which together wrought a metal too heavy to be anything other than this foreboding chain.

(Or launching spring.)

Do you know what it is to be free?

(I do.)

• [The Bridge of Sighs] •

"I can't talk right now."

I know. Can I just sit here until you change your mind?

• [The River Rafts] •

You have so much pent up potential that can either take you somewhere marvelous or disappear in a moment.

Just please remember that. And watch out for nails.

• [The Stars Are Your Headlights] •

I can tell,

she said.

I can tell when

you are floating

in some other place

unsure of color

of time

or space.

You are sailboats

on the horizon.

The offspring of clouds

and whitecaps,

rocking

one another

For when you learn to fly (together)

to sleep

in the wind swept sunshine

and today

is too warm for my

thick wool socks but

I am colder

than my tan

and miss you

too

much.

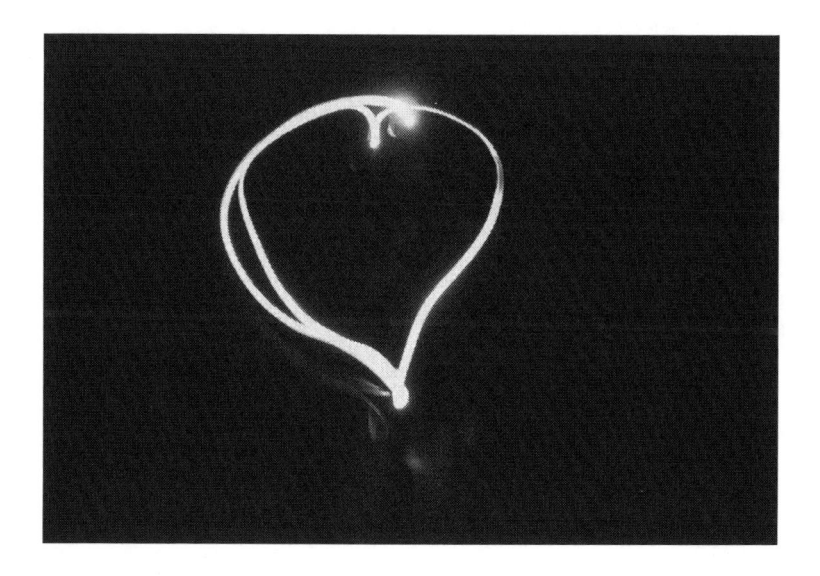

hello, dear one...

• [The No-Longer-In-Kansas] •

They're the kind you see coming from a long way off, stubbornly believing they couldn't possibly hit anywhere close to the beaches of you.

The north wind is their voice and the south their words (both are nothing but air and debris) and the eye of this storm is right when you thought you had succeeded - when you thought you knew the way home.

I understand now why only the biggest storms are named after people.

• [The Things Yesterday's "Someday" Missed] •

1. learning to breathe who you are is the reason that asthma diagnosis was a mistake

2. travel on your own will be one of the least lonely moments of your life, if you see

3. there is a difference between love and confusion and you would be wise to learn how to listen to yourself before you trip over your own toes

4. a contrived poem is no poem at all

5. the morning will say hello in every way it knows how - but yelling is its least favorite, and today was a whisper (just for you)

For when you learn to fly (together)

• [The Hope Chest] •

I can't.

(Yes, you can. You just don't want to.)

It's too hard.

(No, it's not. You're just still hurting.)

Never again.

(Not yet, maybe. And that's okay.)

I don't believe anymore.

(But you will.)

No.

(And until then, I will. For you.)

hello, dear one…

• [The Spoon Wrapped Around My Index Finger Is The Reason I Can Write Today] •

Sometimes

I forget

that I have

hands.

They disappear

like the feeling

of fabric

on skin and

you

next to me

and I am

tired

of feeling

the exact

same

things.

For when you learn to fly (together)

• [The Silence] •

It wasn't about you just being here. Not really. Not unless you were going to say something. Anything.

Care.

(Can you?)

It didn't have to be words.

(I'm still here.)

• [The Long Way 'Round] •

This time, I can breathe. I can hold my own heart in scarred fingers that are no longer ashamed of their lines, for they are roadmaps to the me that I want you to know and I finally know how to walk (again).

• [The Kindest Nothing] •

They said that the most trivial is really that which isn't - lost in the intermediary between dreams and what really happened that night in March, under the full moon and southern stars, to the beating of Kerouac's mad ones - making their way across the battlefield within, digging their trenches in what remains soft in their adventurous soul - preparing themselves to never, never again succumb to the monotonous.

• [The Halcyon Sunshine] •

Sometimes I want to go everywhere and sometimes I want to go nowhere and I sit, here, trying to measure the vastness of each raindrop drifting across my windshield and combining with others and I guess what I'm really trying to say is that I wish I didn't have to go alone.

• [The Pacific Railroad Ties] •

I never asked for you to find these words coherent. I never thought you would analyze them and try to find me in all their corners and white fire. I just hoped you might find, in them, the bits of yourself you forgot.

(I didn't.)

For when you learn to fly (together)

• [The Thank You Note] •

I don't have enough words (I'm not sure I ever could) to tell you how much it means to me (the scales aren't large enough) that you see me (truly, in all my scars) and remind me to hold on (even when my fingers are bleeding, broken, and burned) and keep hoping (even when I need you to hope for me), even when I think I don't matter (but I do).

• [The Being Loved] •

"It's a beautiful thing, is it not?"

Yes.

(Especially when you believe that you are.)

• [The Collaboration] •

We want the sun, and we cannot fly with one wing.

We want the horizon, and we cannot paddle alone.

"So, you're in it together?"

Yes. Because we realize that, if we aren't, a part of us will keep dying. The part that never knew how to breathe in the first place - not until we saw you.

Not until we let

you

see

me.

(Please don't hide anymore.)

• [The Windshield Wipers Ruin The Metaphor] •

The distance between who you are and who you want to be is always more than you think it is, but maybe every moment of growth slowly moves into the next and builds until you're not just walking anymore. Even if there's still a limp.

For when you learn to fly (together)

• [The Sirens Have A Home] •

When you're flying, all the lights below look like they're flickering

Yes no

Hope fear

Joy tears

Every breath of each person within its embrace, and you want to know what I think?

I think they are beautiful.

You.

You are beautiful.

• [The Waking-Up Is The Hardest] •

Maybe not this morning.

but there will be a morning

and it will be beautiful.

I promise.

Just wait until the morning, he said. Wait, and let me dance my fingertips over the still-healing lines you've stopped trying to hide, like they've become your war banner, but really they are white flags. And they whisper about you, I'm sure you know. They say you're a freak and need help, but even if you had three heads I don't know if you'd realize that you already do.

Your bones scream for freedom and you think you're giving it to them - but they're just screaming - for you - the words you think you cannot say.

Try them. Swish these syllables around in your mouth each time you wake up in the morning. Look at yourself in the cracking mirror and watch your lips move with the curves of these letters. Mouth them if you must. Just promise me you'll keep trying.

And then you'll realize that you are Scotland and this fear is England and your defiance is stronger than any oppression could be.

This is for you.

Don't let fear take it.

For when you learn to fly (together)

Don't let anyone take you.

"I am a volcano. About to explode and there's nothing you can do about it. Run. You are Pompeii."

No. I am dolphins giving sailors hope and you are the river that always gets to where it's going - no matter how long it takes.

"Are you the cliffs then?"

No, you don't destroy me. I am only the cliffs when you are the laughing picnickers or peripatetic writer.

"And what if I fall [for you]?"

I'm not worth a crash.

Fly.

• [The Dolphin In My Head] •

And we dance in the hope of the unknown

unwilling to falter or be alone

(though we could.)

We are strong. We are fierce. We are bright.

But together, we are joy.

We soar in water just as swiftly

as eagles over land and our freedom

is not bound

by its own definition.

• [The Wrong Side Of The Bus] •

But I guess it makes sense, doesn't it. I've always been the trees that darken too quickly, wishing I was enough to absorb the sunset like the mountains beyond, because I keep forgetting that my job, instead, is to hold that light. (For you.)

• [The Broken Record] •

I have a tendency to forget sunsets. They're too beautiful to hold in my head forever and so, I let them go. Too soon perhaps.

I forget that people are the same way, lighting up your skies and fading - sometimes - unless you chase them around the horizon like flying west after dusk.

I forget that hugs are important things in life and sometimes letting go is the worst thing you can do to someone.

I have a tendency to forget that I matter [to you].

• [The Sondering] •

He wears plaid shirts and knows three languages - a world traveler with fingerprints in his passport, of all the souls that have walked next to him, but that's as far as they got because his heart doesn't know the words his lips profess. He hides behind the button on his shirt's left front pocket because it's easier than being here - [than admitting that he can't].

He has a med kit in his backpack, extra pens in the top pocket, headphones in his hand, and a flashlight on his keys. He's prepared for anything. But he has never let anyone close enough to hurt him, and the only people he writes to are unmet pen-pals who follow his adventures from a distance, never responding with their own. (He is alone.) He fills his ears with someone else's music, avoiding the rhythm of his own, and the source of his enlightenment is the very thing that blinds him.

He's prepared for everything.

Except you.

(Good.)

Surprise him, with your beautiful conundrum. Challenge him. Be the raindrops on his windshield, knowing that he'll hate these words - at first - until he stops - until he closes his eyes for the first time since her - and breathes - to the beat of your embrace.

And suddenly there's no car anymore. Just him. And you. Skin. And rain. And he welcomes each splash, even

For when you learn to fly (together)

if you're tears today.

Someday he'll be able to hold those too - but today - just keep raining. Until you soak through that plaid shirt's left front pocket and remind his chest what it's like. To feel.

• [The Devouring Threat] •

The waves are coming, dear one.

They will drag you under, confuse your direction, bash you against the rocks, and fill you until you're sputtering for breath and scrambling for the surface.

You can either give in or start swimming. And you'll be faced with this same decision with each subsequent moment.

Keep kicking.

• [The Light Chasers] •

You missed Me, there, in between all the rays of sunlight you thought you were running closer to when I, the Son, was always here next to you - arms outstretched, fingers steady, hoping you would walk, with Me.

• [The True Gift Of Friendship] •

I don't know why we want each other's attention so much. I mean, it couldn't have anything to do with the fact that we're lonely, could it?

Far more likely that you have pieces of my ribs still left on you and we're both in this vindictive quest to either steal those pieces or put them back together.

I think that's what it is. Some people will take. Not even bothering with the courtesy of doing it cleanly. No. It's a snap. It's a break. Leaving shards to grind their way into what was yet untouched.

And then, there are some who will give. They will rip these ribs out of their own chest and give you their lifeblood because - with you - they don't need it anymore.

They're okay, here, knowing that you've finally realized that you matter to someone. Truly. Deeply.

And suddenly neither of you need ribs - no more barriers between your heart and theirs. You, finally, trust.

• [The Mirror That Makes Light Look Dark] •

It amazes me how many times we hide, for fear of being "too much."

Too much of a burden if we tell our story.

Too much of a hassle if we admit we have a need.

Too much pride if we're proud of ourselves, too intimidating if we're confident.

And too much of a waste if we share our hearts.

You are not "too much," dear ones.

You are you.

And you matter.

Don't apologize for that.

• [The Streets Are Filled With Better Things Than Regret] •

We keep looking for validation from the mouths of strangers rather than from those who know us, who love us; for if they knew (and I mean really knew) they couldn't possibly still love. Because we're ugly. We're messed up. We have bruises that we never want anyone to see, from too many nights spent trying to pound ourselves into smoother shapes that don't catch anyone by surprise.

"So what if I told you that you're beautiful anyway?"

That's hard to believe. We look into other people as our warped mirror and can't help but notice that it magnifies our imperfections like a two-way funhouse, never thinking that the view from the other side might be the clearer one.

"You're still beautiful."

• [The Paradox Of Reading] •

These words are mine but they belong to you.

And they breathe so that someday you can too.

(So that someday I can too.)

For when you learn to fly (together)

• [The Turn I'm Glad You Took] •

I don't know if you remember me (I'm not sure why you would. I was that tiny moment in the middle of that one day when you thought there was no way you could possibly heal again), but I remember you.

I remember how your every breath was a cry for help amidst the ashes of hopes that had been poured into a flower mold so that they might be able to pass themselves off as something still alive and breathing.

I remember your voice too. Even though I would never hear it, my ears rang with your aching. And I saw you, dear one. Don't you understand that?

(You were beautiful even then.)

hello, dear one...

• [The Ink Runs Through My Veins] •

And when I can't remember, please remind me.

Grab my fidgeting hands, look me in the eyes, and tell me that the greatest art is lived (not performed) and my "work" will never truly be inspiring if that is all it is.

• [The Texture Of Snow Melt] •

That afternoon - with all its laughter, fog, and silence - stole my frustrations with the assiduous determination of one who has finally found their long lost love and cannot bear the thought of her sadness.

"I am here," He seemed to say. "Take heart."

• [The Mutineer Is You] •

Interesting, isn't it, how we fear to be alone. We surround ourselves with connections, conversations, and camaraderie - thinking they're windows when too often they're just white padding for the walls that keep pressing inward to stifle whatever voice we once had.

"Does it have to be this way?"

No. You can choose to dig instead, broadening tunnels like root systems until you realize that what you're diving through isn't mud.

It's the sun.

For when you learn to fly (together)

• [The Glasses Are Upside-Down] •

People will disappoint you, I can promise you that.

You will have heartbreak and sighs and pen pals who stop responding to your letters, and they'll say to not take it personally when, personally, all I wanted was a friend to care and keep caring.

But people will love you, I can promise you that.

They will love you with hugs and berries and sitting with you, quietly, in the middle of parking lots, on days when you can't even begin to explain why you're just not okay today.

And if you let them, they will help you hope, again.

• [The Cure For Loneliness] •

I searched everywhere, but nobody had a proven vaccine and I couldn't just give you something untested.

(Side effects may include discomfort, laughter, the temporary magnification of symptoms, or hope.)

Be. With someone. Someone who will sit with you and hold your hand and share their strength - to be there as you battle between whether or not it's okay to feel as profoundly as you do.

(Take one daily. Or every hour. Or every third minute on Tuesdays and twice every other day the rest of the week.)

I'd come but, if I'm honest, it scares me sometimes. I don't know how to meet you in your hurts and humanity because they remind me of my own - and I certainly don't deserve to have anyone meet me there. Not in this mess. Not in my burns.

(Continue even after internal symptoms desist.)

And so you took my hand, and filled the cracks of my aches instead of asking me to fill yours.

But we were enough, in that moment, together.

For when you learn to fly (together)

• [The Pop Quiz] •

a) You can be what you want but it may cost more than your purse and I don't think you realize what you're asking for.

b) You can be what they say they want, but I promise you, sooner or later, they'll want something different and will forget about you.

c) You can be different. Defy stereotypes and break down boxes but I'm not sure you'll know what to do, once they're all gone.

d) You can be. And realize that the day got up early to get dressed in sunshine, and it's waiting for you.

Is that enough?

• [The 20 Questions] •

i. I'm still confused as to why we have so many expectations when I thought we said it was okay to be you.

ii. Today was her birthday.

iii. It's not that I've forgotten, it's that I'm choosing to not have to remember.

iv. The world ended last night but it also began again this morning and waking up is its own miracle, if you think about it.

v. It's possible for a stranger to see you more clearly than your friends do and I've learned a lot today, alone.

vi. Next time, please, say my name like it's something more than some town in that state you once passed by on a road trip.

vii. None of the poems I wrote were for you, especially if you have to ask.

viii. I confuse myself sometimes, and most of the time I don't even know where to begin.

ix. I wish you'd stop trying to fix [me].

ix. All I need you to do is tell me that you're here.

ix. Are you going to stay?

ix. (_____).

For when you learn to fly (together)

x. I heard you. I just don't have an answer, today.

xi. I'm the one who switched out your coffee for decaf last night because I didn't have the energy to go out, either.

xii. Once, I spent the whole day listening to the same song on repeat and I didn't even notice I had headphones in.

xiii. I pass the same cafe every day and I've always wanted to go in but now, after 17 days of "eh, tomorrow maybe" and 16 of forgetting, I'm strangely afraid to walk in and say hello.

xiv. Maybe I understand now why the old man two doors down sits at the same park bench every morning at 10:07, even if it's raining.

xv. Change is scary and if I stop traveling I start to remember why.

xvi. Dorothy was right, with or without the ruby red slippers.

xvii. I forgot how to like my own handwriting.

xviii. Some of my scars still hurt and I don't say anything because I'm afraid you might actually understand.

xix. Yes.

xx. Not if I have to explain it all, again.

hello, dear one…

FOR WHEN YOU FALL (AGAIN)

hello, dear one…

• [The Tears On Fifth Street] •

You know that feeling when you stand in the same place every day, looking at the same view, thinking each morning that it's going to disappear today because it couldn't possibly last forever and, let's be honest, your faith isn't quite big enough to believe it'll stay?

Yeah… Me neither.

(Please stay.)

• [The Ribcage's Secrets] •

Sometimes the only sign I have that you're still living is the soft rustle of fabric as you breathe and it scares me to be out of earshot.

• [The White Fire Needs The Black] •

Just because people are more likely to read between the lines than hear your words doesn't mean that you should stop.

All the paper in the world means nothing without your ink.

• [The Dance Card We Keep Filling] •

I'm just still in that mode where things make sense because they don't make sense. So don't mind me. I'll just be here writing until my pen has had enough and my heart knows that these, these words, they mattered.

"They do. They matter. Because they're yours."

And someday I will believe that.

• [The Loan Shark] •

I am water. I am waves. I am the ocean that cannot escape its own depths no matter how many times it breaks - pulled backwards as much as it is shoved forward into a land that does not welcome it.

And so I will keep crashing upon this sunset shore, trusting that, soon, my droplets will refract enough gold to pay off your fear.

For when you fall (again)

• [The Screams Lessen] •

It's easy.

You just wake up and say, "today I will let go. Today this won't hurt me anymore".

And then you fail and fall asleep.

We'll try again tomorrow.

• [The Choir's Sermon] •

Look. You need to understand that the world is going to tell you "no" and hold you down with every ounce of its strength. You're going to have to keep remembering that the world is a feather and you are a mountain.

I'm not going to try to tell you that every step forward is easier than the one before. Sometimes the 700th stair is way worse than the 40th, and still the way seems unending but, gosh, you are so beautiful.

And you stand higher than the rest.

• [The Apathy Of Dying] •

I don't have the heart for this. I would rather drown. Exposed. All the life bursting out of me into something useful for the rest of the world and that reminds them they can still breathe.

(Why is it so hard to breathe sometimes?)

I don't want to fade.

For when you fall (again)

• [The Funhouse Mirrors Are Held By Friends Sometimes] •

There will come a time when you will feel the most truly "you" you have ever felt. And then someone you love will say that you're not. And you're going to have to decide which voice to listen to.

But it's okay to just be quiet, dear one. And let your heart remind you why you wanted to be true to it in the first place.

• [The Prescription] •

"Why do you write?"

Where do you find the strength to not have to?

• [The Odd Thing About Coming Home] •

If you keep

thinking

it's the same tide

every time

in and out

you'll forget

that your

pocket pebbles

are smoother

than before

and it's easier

to carry them

now.

(I know you.)

For when you fall (again)

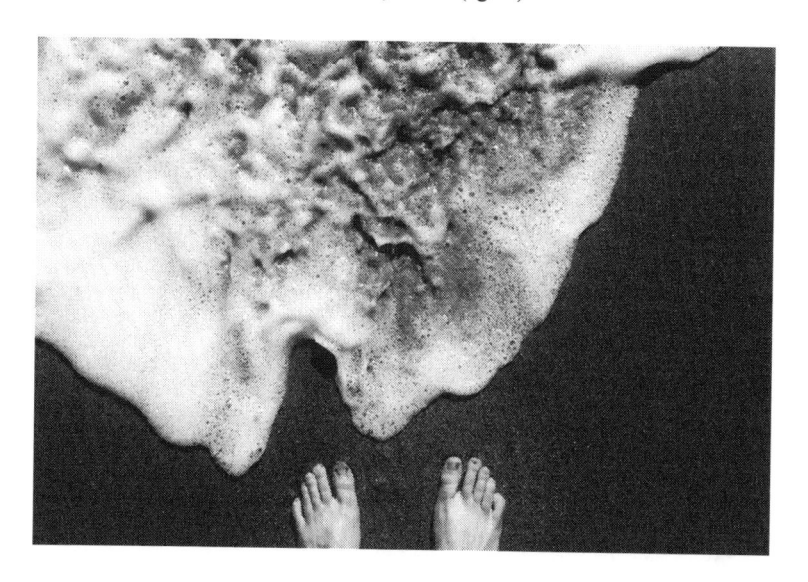

• [The Waves That Try To Trap Us] •

I know how it goes. And then there are those sleepless nights that plague you even after you awaken. And it's all you can do to find your pulse and thereby remind yourself that you are alive. Even when every part of you screams that you shouldn't be.

But that is the biggest lie anyone could ever tell you.

Please hear this.

That. Is. A. Lie.

You are the note that makes us a harmony. You are the aroma that makes this rose special. You are the footsteps that make ours a symphony.

And you are ALIVE.

Please stay with me.

• [The Beautiful Curse] •

I am the puddle by the bus stop that you sit at each morning, waiting; watching the pattern of the raindrops make their little splashes, and you wonder if they sting.

They do. Sometimes. All the time. Only when I think about it.

These thoughts and feelings pelt and pepper me, some more forceful than others, but all with the same deep intention to either become part of me or leave something in their wake. And I can choose to either listen to their beautiful sound or feel like I'm getting soaked to the skin and not even the umbrella is helping. Gosh, not even this umbrella is helping and it really stinks here sometimes; here by the roadway, on those cobblestone sidewalks you love so much, stepped in or splashed through (does it matter if it's intentional or not?), until those moments in between when the sun breaks through from the horizon and - even though it's still raining - each drop refracts a rainbow of it's own and I'm reminded how beautiful this truly is:

To feel.

For when you fall (again)

• [The Theses Of My Veins] •

How many times do I have to bleed this before you realize that you are utterly

preciously

incredibly

completely

loved?

• [The Raw And Unapologetic] •

I'm lost here. Often. Much more often than I ever really admit to anyone.

My head is a maze: sometimes the kid-sized one where you can step over the walls to get to where you need to go and can see the end the whole way; sometimes the dark, stranglingly-narrow hedges that tower over your head and turn way more often than you imagine possible for the short distance you thought you were going.

I fight. Most of the time. I struggle my way through or around and usually into the thicket before I find a shortcut out that scratches several layers below the skin. But I get out. And I'm stronger.

And then sometimes I can't. And I sit in the middle of it all and, to you, it may look like a peaceful garden. My skin is unscathed, my hem still clean, but I'm not here. Look closer, someday, please. Don't go by when you wonder if I'm okay. You might just see that my eyes have taken on the hues of the hedges themselves and realize that I can't see beyond them anymore - until you somehow convince me to take your hand, or to at least believe that the green is still beautiful.

(It used to be my favorite color).

For when you fall (again)

• [The Fashion Of Inkwells] •

I'm tripping over my own words like running in heels on a mountainside when all I needed to do was sit there and be.

"Did you even notice the sunset tonight?"

• [The Sunburn] •

Even the Sahara was once under water so really, you can't tell me you've always been like this.

(You can't tell me you've always wanted to be numb.)

• [The Silence Of Music] •

No, you don't get it. I hear too much. Cars and birds and yelling and smiles; tapping fingernails and sighs and my own thoughts (and all of them); and you (and your pain) and I don't mind (I love it) but sometimes, gosh darn it, I hear too much, and I just need loud headphones to find quiet (to remember why it's beautiful, to hear).

• [The Day That Didn't Exist] •

Every moment that ever existed [between two people] can either be a blessing or a regret. I know that. And I hate being stuck between the two.

"But you learned something, didn't you?"

Yeah. I learned that, too often, we say "I miss you" when we really mean "I miss who I was before you."

"Do you really mean that?"

Yes. And no. I'm better now, I know, but I don't want to be convinced that it took you to get me here and the closest I can get to "smiling because it happened" is the grimace of those who cannot forget.

"Why do you want to? Forget, I mean."

Hearts are the thing I never wanted to break.

"Is the rebuilding beautiful?"

You know, it is. And more so because I know what it

For when you fall (again)

took to start at the base, removing broken bricks and cracked concrete and seeing what my hands can do. They bled though. A lot. You can't imagine how many shards I had to remove and re-melt.

"Do they still hurt?"

No. They're callused now. I don't even notice the pain.

"Oh, but can they still feel? Have the shards cut your nerves and dulled even the sensation of softness?"

It's better this way.

"No, it's not."

Are you trying to tell me that the good is worth the pain? Because I don't want to go back.

"Yes. It is. Please believe me. It's beautiful."

• [The Lost In Translation] •

They say

I am

writing.

But I am really

just trying

to

breathe.

• [The Value Of Nursery Rhymes] •

There's a weight on my chest and it thrums like the ABC's.

A, B, breathe like somehow, for this instance, you're able to reach the sea's depths and let it become a part of,

C, D, E, everything all at once like a hammer into the soul.

F, G, H, I never thought it would be this way,

J, K, L, love is not the answer, it is the questions. It is the dot at the bottom of the exclamation mark that only half of writers know the name of but less than few can explain the reason why it doesn't matter whether we remember or not.

For when you fall (again)

M, N, O, over the years I've forgotten why we're chasing something we don't even understand.

P, Q, R, did you really mean it when you said hello?

S, I still remember when you knew how to smile.

T, Time isn't going to be enough, or don't you know that yet?

U, you need to decide.

V, W, whether you're going to keep believing this lie that's stuck to the inside of your ribs but this

X, x-ray shows the truth of it's impermanence.

Y, Z, no, read it again. I will keep singing this song like a broken record until it's the only refrain you can hear - until it drowns out that lie and lets your heartbeat take over conducting again.

• [The Sliding Door Won't Open With A Push] •

Look, I'm going to need you to take a step back and calm down. Stop slamming all your weight into something that won't budge. Stop screaming inside your own heart. And, for goodness sake, stop panicking.

You are trapped only by your own desperation and if you stopped, for a second, to breathe, you'd realize the truth.

(You're okay.)

• [The Flour Under Her Fingernails] •

I wish

I could tell you

why I don't want to tell you

that what I did today was sit

alone

at the café by my house,

watching cloudless storms

motionless mania

and empty chairs,

headphones playing

For when you fall (again)

their loudest silence

until the yeast-less bread

rises

and I can finally

go

home.

"So what did you do today?"

Nothing.

(Everything.)

• [The Unwritten Rule] •

We've been fed a reflection so often that we've come to define it as perfection and forget that even the smallest touch can distort it all.

So we don't touch. We don't go. We don't see.

We hide behind this subconscious fear of ruining something that we simultaneously believe is flawless.

"Illogical," you say, but our hearts know the truth.

We were made for something more than this.

• [The Minotaur's Cousin] •

And what if we are realizing that somewhere, deep down, there's a coward living that we never wanted the world to meet, and so we keep planting ourselves on tall places to prove it wrong.

But it lives. And these rocks cannot topple the Jericho we have built to hide it from the world.

And now we're the ones struggling to get out.

For when you fall (again)

• [The Definition That Was Never Yours To Write] •

Note to self:

Every time you said, "it couldn't possibly get better than this," it did.

So then why do you keep believing that you don't matter, when even the most beautiful things in life are drawn to you?

You are not the sun, setting vibrantly and leaving darkness. You are the horizon it longs to dive into, knowing that in you it finds a new beginning.

• [The Grip Of The Brink] •

"There are two sides to every story," she reminds me emphatically. "Even to our own," but that shouldn't make sense. It shouldn't make sense that we struggle within ourselves (is my perspective not my own?) to do something even as infinitesimal (and important) as get out of bed in the morning (or believe that we matter in this world).

"Come on, now. Take a step. Now another." (The door isn't getting any closer!)

My own voice says to let go - as it wraps around me and pulls backward (I really don't think that's fair). And the same voice says keep on - as it slices through those vines (please don't hit me!)

"Well, which side is winning? The fighter or the doubter?"

Whichever side is holding on.

"Is it over yet?"

No, I'm not.

• [The Rest Of Tomorrow] •

You will walk again. And when you do, you will wonder why you ever thought you failed.

• [The Filter-Perfect Life] •

I wish I could go back to the day they started telling you to do more. Be more. Be stronger. Hold it all together. Succeed - on our standards. Hide everything we deem lesser in the envelope filled with all the letters you'll never send because you're afraid of what love might actually mean. Hold on to nothing and it won't fail you (like you constantly fail us). And then, when you think you're there, come back. Start over. (Good luck.)

I wish I would have told you, then, how beautiful you are.

(Are you still here?)

Will you let me love you, again?

• [The Petition] •

I need you to live.

I need you to disentangle your limbs from the sphere you've made of yourself just to take up less space in this world, throw open your hands, and I need you to scream.

I need you to feel that ferocity of life bubbling up inside you once more, mentos in a coke bottle, except this time not fizzing out. You are perpetual. You are living. And if that is not enough for you then keep screaming.

Yell with every fiber of your being. Yell out the trepidity in your toes, the nightmares in your knees. Yell out the sadness in your stomach, loneliness in your lungs, and every bit of the hurt still clawing its way through your heart like a poison blackening your veins into a roadmap of warped words. And yell out the stillness. Until you realize that you're still moving.

I need you to live.

Please.

And I will say this. Again. Hoping each time is a sledgehammer chipping away at the soundproof walls you've constructed around the heart that I love so much. And I will keep fighting. Until this truth finally breaks through and you hear me.

I need you to live.

• [The Heartbeats Are Proof] •

Please don't let anyone convince you that you're not enough.

You are so much more than the world gets to see.

And you matter.

• [The Confusion] •

I think it's my responsibility to remind you that, here in the fog, everything looks the same and all we have to keep us together are fingertips.

But I'll use mine to tap promises into your palms on every step, just in case you start to forget.

• [The Time I Caught Myself Dreaming] •

What if I could write one poem, and it would save somebody's life?

What if I am a poem.

Could I save you?

• [The Way Bitterness Takes Hold] •

They say that the constant sound of the wind is enough to drive you mad; that its constant whistling and battering against windows and men alike slowly creep into the mind until they're all you can hear. Until neither earplugs nor music can drown out the unrelenting threat of cold.

It seeps into the body this way: through the mind. Until you're cold from the inside out rather than the other way around.

• [The Coin Spinning In The Donation Funnel] •

It's really just a trick, you know - make something so interesting to watch that people are willing to give just to see it again. Slowly. Around. Faster. Smaller. Dizzying. And then it's gone before you realize you were too distracted to save yourself from the fall.

For when you fall (again)

• [The Security Blanket] •

You wear the fog like a shield, thinking it'll help soften the harshness of a world that's too often black and white, overturned angles against a blank sky, and plastic flowers on Valentine's Day.

But you see, the thing is, you're still here. You're still breathing. And with every one of those breaths, I hope you are reminded, again and again, that the world is softer than you believe it to be.

(You are stronger than you believe yourself to be.)

And I still think you're beautiful.

• [The Hope That Lies in You] •

"You don't have to be scared."

But how?

How can you be so sure that the waves won't take me down with them? How can you know that these days won't become all I know? How do you know that they're not too strong?

"Because I Am."

• [The Fog Chasers] •

It's the fourth step that's the hardest.

The first one feels like stepping into a cloud, until it embraces you in the second and after the third you begin to forget where you are.

Left is up and right is upside down and I really can't explain to you which way I'm going anymore.

But I've learned to love that uncertainty. Somehow. And once I did, I found you. In a place I would never have looked.

Sometimes it takes getting lost to make us realize we were all along.

For when you fall (again)

• [The Dawn Doesn't Apologize] •

"Just watch the sun, please, dear one. And then someday you will look around and realize that I'm still here no matter how many times you didn't believe it."

• [The Shadow Isn't Stronger] •

No matter how much the past taunts. No matter how loudly the future yells. And no matter how ferociously the present burns. We came into this world in defiance of all the illogical "I can'ts" and we will continue the same way; for our possibilities far outweigh the world's doubts and we were made for this. This, and so much more.

(Don't let go.)

• [The Unseen Tree Still Falls] •

Can we stop asking whether you'll be heard or not and acknowledge that you still feel? And this hurts. I don't care how many people aren't there to see it.

But I need you to know that someone sees you. Even when you can't see yourself.

Please. Don't let go.

• [The Boiling Frog Is You] •

I'm not afraid of falling. I'm afraid of standing still for so long that I forget how to breathe and turn into a monument to all the impossibilities and chains of painful pasts.

(I don't get it. How can you forget to breathe? That's not possible!)

Oh, but it is. You wrap yourself in a blanket of fears - comfortable enough to distract you from the fact that the air in here is becoming stagnant and you convince yourself that you don't need it anymore; that the glare of that sun is too much.

(I'm too much.)

No, you're not.

Keep moving.

Don't you dare stop.

For when you fall (again)

• [The Lunar Eclipse] •

And then we realize we'd rather be bleeding, for we can watch the outside heal. No matter how slow, we see change. But this? This indescribable ache haunts us inside. This grief we cannot describe writhes its way into our depths as if to burrow were its only purpose and the eye cannot see it wither. (Is it withering?) But it does. (Yes.) It's dying. It's dying and you are not, no matter how many times your heart may tell you otherwise - it is still pumping. You are still feeling. Your fingers still move, your heart still beats (unsteady sometimes, but that's okay), and your lungs are too. It doesn't matter if you're struggling right now.

This is not forever, dear one.

Hold on.

(And I will too.)

• [**The Boots That Aren't Made For Walking (This Far)**] •

You could spend the rest of your life worrying about breaking things, if you'd like. Leave them on the shelf, pristine and untouched, but I promise you, eventually, you'll forget why you have them in the first place.

(Get up.)

Use them. Wear them out. Love them and scuff them and scratch them and run and slip and fall and get back up again because this is what you was made for and none of these "things" shall define you.

(Your heart can handle it.)

• [**The Darkness Visible (Amongst The Stars)**] •

And if it wasn't there, would you even notice the galaxies all around?

For when you fall (again)

• [The Distance Between Us Isn't Measured In Years] •

You saying you're not enough is not humility. Not like this. It is poison.

You self-deprecating, beautiful soul.

Don't you know how brightly you shine?

• [The Oasis Is Closer Than You Think] •

The strongest moments feel so far removed from the floods that you might as well be in a desert, but please don't stay there. Don't hide. Don't become so isolated that your very skin becomes the brittle edges of beloved manuscripts still cherished, but so liable to break.

Stay close, dear ones. Please.

• [The Pebble On The Edge Of The Tide] •

"I'm not like them," she says. "Not colorful, not unique; just grey on this shore and not even the sunset can make me shine."

No. You're just afraid (though I'm not quite sure why) to let yourself be pulled back into the hope you were shaped by in the first place (and it misses you.)

• [The Bad Day] •

You woke up again today.

Your heart hasn't forgotten its rhythm (even in this race with your thoughts to see which one will define you) and your lungs decided to keep doing their job (through the haze, in spite of the weight, above the waves).

And somebody loves you.

So tell me again why today isn't a good enough reason to smile.

• [The Last Glimpse Of Fear] •

I'm not entirely convinced that what we need is to be noticed.

I think we just need to be told it's okay to feel.

• [The Photosynthesis Of People] •

"They would never do that to me."

You're right. But you are. To yourself. Because you can't seem to let go of whatever hurt seems bigger than the sun today.

• [The Sidewalk Strangers Are My Philharmonic] •

"There are times it would be easier if my mind was sedated and my soul didn't know hurt."

I don't think you believe that, deep down. I don't think you're truly lost enough for that. But it hurts, I get it. You see the stories of people around you (sometimes better than they can themselves) and you hold them. You feel the pain buried in their unbroken bones that might as well be shards for how often they threaten to drive themselves into hearts and lungs and break their rhythm. The rhythm that steadies the song of their lives. But it wavers. It skips. And with imperfect hearing you memorize the songs that they have yet to hear.

But you hope. You hope that someday they will see how important their harmony is, and that the apparent dissonance and imperfections are nothing more than the masterful movements of a Conductor who understands that resolution doesn't have to make sense until the last measure. And it certainly doesn't have to be in C major.

(I love your song too.)

For when you fall (again)

• [The Passage I Always Need To Underline] •

I am still breathing, in fact. And my smile is just as authentic. If I appear otherwise, it is merely my own questions on top of a fear that I refuse to succumb to and my head will not sink unless in sleep or prayer.

I will be.

I will breathe.

I will loose my anxious grip on the pen of my own life and trust that the ink's fade is momentary.

I am okay.

I know myself.

My wings are getting stronger. I will not be buried again.

I will soar.

hello, dear one...

FOR WHEN YOU SOAR

hello, dear one...

• [The Fight Within Is A Dance] •

I am heavy.

No I'm not.

I am light.

No, I'm certainly not.

I am a blended mix between the two of all my pain and joy and blood and yet still, somehow, You are light. You are light in and through me, around and before, and my greatest pain is the biggest thing that winds us both together.

I am Yours.

• [The Dissertations Of Folly] •

Between the present and the future lie the shadows of the people you could have been and, if you let them, they will taunt you. They will line up their arguments like theses pounded into the doorframe of your soul until you yourself shake with the resonance of mistakes.

Don't listen. Don't let them tell you you're too broken to keep breathing.

You're not. You never will be. And to believe them is to negate the beauty of who you are now.

You shine so much brighter than shadows.

"And are you shining, or do you feel like a shadow?"

I will always shine. Even when parts of me feel like they can't. The shadow will never be all of me.

"I see both parts. That's why I know you're beautiful. Because you never give up."

• [The Petals Of Lost Books] •

I am made of pieces, and we fight over whether I am greater than their sum or if they own me.

But I am more than my binding. And the epilogue is just the beginning of volume two.

(Don't stop writing.)

• [The Out-Of-Office Auto Reply] •

I'll be away from these fears for the duration of my stay [in Your arms] but leave a message and I'll get back to these when I can [tell them apart from the truth].

Sincerely [done doing this on my own],

Me.

• [The Asphalt Canvas] •

It's not enough for me to hear the rain anymore. I need to feel it, beating, lifting out all of the memories that I've tried (and failed) to forget and releasing them into something that can shine again.

I need to feel them: running down my arms like forgotten marbles that keep playing their game because they know they're beautiful, even if I have forgotten them like hope and childlike excitement; culminating in droplets on my fingers that grow, slowly; and fall, splashing. Becoming emblems of my freedom.

I am alive. This reminds me. In all of the moments when I can't remember on my own, I am reminded by the falling rain that welcomes me into its embrace and says I can be one of them too.

But I swear, if I am one droplet then I am seven. I am twelve. I am buckets. I am a fire hose. I am an explosion of life that can no sooner be held back than this cloud can be closed up by a simple chiding.

I am alive.

• [The Parapets Of You] •

"And I could have sworn that she was weightless; there, with her barefoot soul tracing patterns on the sands of my skin but I'm too close - too blinded - to read."

• [The Day Your Blood Type Changed] •

You will have hard days. You will have those ones when just getting up is a struggle and everything feels like weight on top of an already burdened soul.

But you will also have these days: when first meetings turn to friendships, laughter writes the memories, and your skin absorbs both sunrise and sunset and weaves the rays into the lining of you until all you can do is shine.

And the hard days cannot take this.

No; the hard days cannot even compete. For even in pain, you bleed light. And that is the most beautiful thing.

(Don't forget.)

• [The Calendar Is A Puzzle] •

It's just another day, in just another coffee shop down the street, with wooden tables and not-her-favorite-pastry (because somebody else ordered the last one) and splattered paint on the floor beneath her too-worn boots - messy, on accident; beautiful, defiantly - with muddy runs in thunderstorms, Jesus talks with strangers and counting raindrops on windowsills.

It was a Tuesday. Her favorite day of the week, because nobody ever gives a second glance to Tuesdays and she can't stand the thought of moments being hoarded in a dragon's lair when there are so many out there who would do anything for one of them - even to just see its shine - once.

It's just

another

day.

But Tuesdays are her favorite because her feet are still trying to learn the week's rhythm and she'll trip if she doesn't pay attention - if she forgets to see.

It's just

another

Tuesday.

But Tuesdays are her favorite. Because nobody really remembers what you do on a Tuesday, so there's really no pressure to convince anybody else that your day was spectacular. (This is for you.)

It's "just another day..." if you want it to be.

(Not to me, it isn't.)

• [The Reason] •

...Art is vulnerable. It is strong. It is overcoming this fear of "can't" with all the determination of "try" and the realization that we are our own worst critics – and we will never fully believe that our art matters until we realize that we do...

|| Full poem on soundcloud.com/sweeterchord ||

• [The Texture Of Plane Windows] •

I don't know what poems they write about me. But I hope they don't rhyme. I hope they alliterate spontaneously and coincide syllabically only occasionally. I hope they make you feel. Cry, if you must, or scream to the wind. I don't really mind at this point.

I just hope my life made you feel something.

If it didn't, I really don't know why else you'd read it.

• [The Pinholes In My Lampshade] •

I tried to catch a piece of light every day. I tried to keep them for you in the mason jar behind my teapot and when people asked what they were, I would just say "Wait."

But my fingers are made of scars and not star dust. So all I have are memories and little moments and I hope you someday see that they are the stars.

• [The Space Around The Stars] •

The funny thing about light is that dark doesn't make it harder to see. It makes it shine.

• [The Storm's Eye Is A Mirror] •

Sometimes the beautiful chaos of our own hearts breaks into the light and we're stunned by all the possibility wrought into something so simple.

And yet you're still seeing monochrome when your heart is colors that haven't even been named.

• [The First Mate's Log] •

Being all of who you are and doing all of what you can do are not equivalent concepts. And I'd rather have the former than be out here, sails flying high, in a boat that's taking on water, too fast.

• [The Things That Do Not Matter] •

Don't listen to them.

Find a corner. Find a park bench. Find a bar to lean against on the subway to steady your hand. Find the smile of the beggar woman on the street corner after a stranger gives her an apple. Find the sliver of light that peeks through your window at 8:23am, precisely.

And write.

Write the way the crack in the blue tile matches the scar across your palm from likewise straining to hold these walls in place. Write the way the elderly couple on the next bench over have developed their own language after 42 years of marriage and how everything has changed but their eyes. Write the way the commuters move with the train, like steps of a dance only they know the rhythm to. Write the way it feels to be seen.

Write that light. Because when it disappears at 8:26am, precisely, I want you to still remember (that I see you).

• [The Word To The Wise] •

Be.

Yes, that's the only word I have for you. No, it's not a mistake. I'm fully aware of the fact that you tend to get wrapped up in your complicated wisdom and forget the simplicity of this world.

(Don't forget Me.)

• [The Fear Of Missing Out] •

Understand this: the day you stop begging for somedays is the day you can realize that you've already begun living them - you merely forgot to say thank you.

• [The "Normal" Day] •

"So have you figured it out yet? Why it's okay to be you?"

Well, I know the reason should be "because I matter." But I think, today, it's just "because it is."

Because it's enough to go on a café-hunt and feel weird sitting at a barrel table and get asked out by an old man who thinks you look very alone, there in the plaza, while you write poetry and watch the sunlight trace leaves on the sidewalk.

(Because living is not a waste of time.)

• [The Tree Outside Of The Forest Is My Favorite] •

If there's one thing I've learned from you, it's that it's okay to stand out. It's okay to be different, spectacular, and not make sense. It's okay to defy the odds, break stereotypes, and confuse the world.

It's okay to be yourself.

"Believe that."

Okay.

• [The Autumn Leaves] •

We're small. Tiny, really; essentially imperceptible splashes of color on a canvas that stretches across a universe of maybes and potentials and threatens to never end - but, damn it, don't you understand how beautiful you are? I know I can't see this whole canvas (it'd be overwhelming if I could..) but even a peek is enough to send me spiraling from speechless wonder to misunderstood conceptions of insignificance.

(Do I even matter?)

And then I look at you. I see how magnificently your color contrasts with the canvas behind you and I wonder if, maybe, without us, monochromatic would weep.

• [The Soul's Front Is Not All Quiet] •

I don't know these people; these faceless souls next to me in the trenches, yelling out their fury toward a world that hurts itself, and yet still fighting for it. For the people behind us. And they are beautiful.

They are beautiful, and I have not met them yet, but we will fight together. And keep fighting. With paint and words and still-wet pages written in our own red ink because we used up all the rest and you are worth it. You are worth that simple gift, even if you never believe me.

We will keep fighting for you. Together. Because you matter. And your story is enough reason for us to keep the demons at bay.

We don't need recognition. No thank you cards, no speeches.

Just live. Do that for me, will you? Until you learn to keep living for yourself and for something bigger.

And keep fighting.

(You might be someone's trench warrior someday.)

• [The Battlements] •

You're not burning because of the sun. You're burning because your own light is turning this armor into an oven when the rest of us are here just hoping for a moment of that warmth.

Maybe then you'd remember who you were before you put it on.

• [The Ant Colony Effect] •

You have to remember. You have to figure out how to step off of this gridlocked freeway, filled with beings that do nothing more than crowd the highway (inside your own mind), and somehow remember that numbers in no way diminish the significance of you.

• [The Introduction] •

I know you. You and your helping hands and steady feet and strong shoulders. You and your concerned eyes and ready ears and grace filled heart.

You and your age-old scars and still-healing bruises and broken songs. You and your stillness.

I love you.

(All of you.)

• [The Space Between The Lines] •

There are words reaching out from within you, clamoring to be heard amidst every other voice that's vying for your dwindling margin.

But I want you to realize that they're important. Because your voice is important, dear one.

So write. Speak. Dance. Paint. Go do!

And if you need me, I'll be here. And we can smear ink on our hands and trust that the curves of our fingerprints know which story to tell.

Even when we don't.

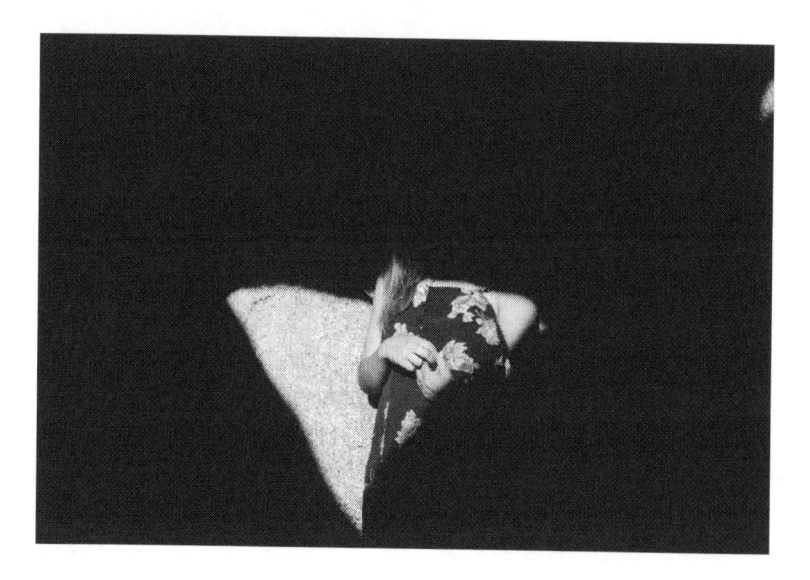

• [The Truest Birthday Gift] •

It's not that I want to convince you that you are loved. It's that I want to be your reminder - today and whenever you need it (even if you don't think you do) - that you already were. Utterly. Completely. Incessantly and perfectly. By the One who called you "Beloved" before time began.

(You need this too, dear one.)

Yes. I need other people.

And that's okay, too.

• [The Unselfishness Of Candlelight] •

I've never met anyone else who can simultaneously stand and move as beautifully as you do. You're astounding.

You, somehow, fit your own pain into the warmth that heals; your own breath into the light that makes these moments make sense. You are the only one who can silently scream "THIS MATTERS" and make me actually believe it.

You hope for this more for me than you do for yourself, and that's both beautiful and hard. You and your stubborn, silent strength; bearing a hurt wrapped in a shroud of the love you give out to others without hesitation. Without saving some for yourself.

But, dear one, your mistake is thinking that you still have to carry this hurt you're so desperate to hide. Sometimes letting it go doesn't mean giving it to the world. It just means letting it go.

• [The Moment After Midnight] •

I am more than just the scars I've borne.

I am here, and I am strong enough to stay.

(I'll see you tomorrow.)

• [The Marble Caves] •

I used to fear my dreams. I would refuse to share them and almost not even admit them to myself.

But then I learned to chase them. And I found the dearest friends to run after them with me and remind me to never stop hoping.

That, for me, is this moment.

For when you help someone else realize their dreams, you notice that maybe, all along, they were the ones helping you realize yours.

• [The Ones That Escape The Jar] •

I am not butter

with soaked wings

waiting

to fly.

I am

upside down

fire-

spinning,

tumbling,

light filling the

sky.

I am more than what you said I could ever be.

• [The Dizzying Heights] •

You are yesterday's child, today's accomplishment, and tomorrow's dream. So tell me why you can't find it within yourself to keep breathing.

"It isn't always that easy."

I know. (But we need you.)

• [The Smoke In My Head
(That Keeps Me From Seeing)] •

You will need them, don't forget that. You'll need the store clerk smiles. You will need the mom hugs and the friend high fives; the father laughs and the best friend secret handshakes. You will even need the waves from corner people that you may never see again (but, for that instant, you saw one another).

So remember.

Remember that even the smallest recognitions of life are an oasis.

(And you were never the desert to me.)

• [The Sound Of Breathing Played Backwards] •

If you're close enough

if you listen

if you're willing

(if you stay)

you will hear me

quietly

(screaming)

silently,

every other minute,

"shut up"

"you don't define me"

"I won't listen"

"not anymore"

• [The Silence Forgot You] •

Don't try to be quiet. Don't try to silence yourself when you were meant to be a brilliant flare of life casting away shadows from the corners of every life you come into contact with. You're brilliant, you know. In the truest sense. Sending light farther than you ever thought you could reach on your own, until it returns to the sun from whence it came - not equal, but more - having translated hope through the hundreds of souls [you never met] but still have one thing to say.

Thank you.

• [The Christening] •

"You are the same," said the voices, "when everything around you is different. New. Whole. Rejoicing. But you? You are the same. You are stuck."

No.

I am new every morning, whole again each moment, and I will not believe their lies again.

This is for You

• [The Heart Forgave You First] •

Okay.

Let me tell you something.

You will reach a moment

when nothing makes sense

and your heart

feels like it's outside

your chest

clamoring

clawing

its way back

into the safety

of you,

and you're just there,

screaming,

silently,

"how can you possibly

trust me

this much?"

(Because I know you.)

(Because I love you.)

hello, dear one...

• [The Coin Amongst The Pebbles] •

Sometimes it hits me

that it hasn't yet fully hit me

how beautiful it is

to be able to trust.

God. Myself. My friends. And you.

To trust is a choice.

To trust is a gift.

To trust is a beautiful invitation to deeper and deeper hope and,

I've learned,

all the pain of the past cannot overshadow hope and,

I know

(now)

that I've always been strong enough for this.

(Somehow.)

Because You are.

For when you soar

• [The Epilogue] •

Nice try. I know you're reading ahead. And I'm not going to spoil the middle for you. Just know that you are loved.

And you're going to be okay.

hello, dear one...

INDEX

hello, dear one...

Index

The 20 Questions	60
The Ant Colony Effect	117
The Apathy Of Dying	68
The Asphalt Canvas	106
The Autumn Leaves	56
The Bad Day	96
The Battlements	117
The Beautiful Curse	72
The Being Loved	43
The Boiling Frog Is You	92
The Boots That Aren't Made For Walking (This Far)	94
The Bravery Of Hearing	17
The Breath In The Fog	30
The Bridge of Sighs	35
The Broken Record	49
The Bruises On Our Knuckles	11
The Calendar Is A Puzzle	108
The Choir's Sermon	68
The Christening	126
The Clifftop Is A Cave	14
The Coin Amongst The Pebbles	128
The Coin Spinning In The Donation Funnel	88
The Collaboration	44
The Confusion	87
The Cure For Loneliness	58
The Dance Card We Keep Filling	66
The Darkness Visible (Amongst The Stars)	94
The Dawn Doesn't Apologize	91
The Dawn In Me	12
The Day That Didn't Exist	76
The Day You Screened Darkness' Call	13

hello, dear one...

The Day Your Blood Type Changed	107
The Definition That Was Never Yours To Write	83
The Devouring Threat	51
The Dichotomies In My Head	12
The Dictionary Is Incomplete	34
The Difference Today	32
The Dissertations Of Folly	104
The Distance Between Us Isn't Measured In Years	95
The Dizzying Heights	122
The Dolphin In My Head	48
The Dream Quilt	8
The End Of Tomorrow	16
The Epilogue	129
The Faceless Mirror	17
The Fashion Of Inkwells	75
The Fear Of Missing Out	113
The Fight Within Is A Dance	103
The Filter-Perfect Life	85
The First Mate's Log	111
The Flour Under Her Fingernails	80
The Fog Chasers	90
The Funhouse Mirrors Are Held By Friends Sometimes	69
The Game Gravity Plays	33
The Glasses Are Upside-Down	57
The Grammatically Correct Way To Be Crazy	32
The Grip Of The Brink	84
The Halcyon Sunshine	42
The Heart Forgave You First	126
The Heart Grew Three Sizes Today	34
The Heart Is Precious. (Don't Forget)	29
The Heartbeats Are Proof	87

Index

The Hope Chest	39
The Hope That Lies in You	90
The Ink Doesn't Have To Go On Paper	12
The Ink Runs Through My Veins	56
The Instruction Manual Is Missing (All Its) Pages	29
The Introduction	118
The Kindest Nothing	42
The Last Glimpse Of Fear	97
The Letters She Wrote Were To Herself	3
The Lies That Fog The Mirror	6
The Light Chasers	52
The Light That Knows You Better Than The Dark Places	16
The Littlest Phoenix	iii
The Loan Shark	66
The Long Way 'Round	41
The Longest Tunnel	20
The Lost In Translation	78
The Lunar Eclipse	93
The Marble Caves	121
The Marvelous Ones	5
The Minotaur's Cousin	82
The Mirror That Makes Light Look Dark	53
The Misunderstanding Effect	19
The Moment After Midnight	115
The Mutineer Is You	56
The Newness	30
The No-Longer-In-Kansas	38
The "Normal" Day	114
The Oasis Is Closer Than You Think	95
The Odd Thing About Coming Home	70
The One That Remains	4

hello, dear one...

The One You Skipped	10
The Ones That Escape The Jar	122
The Other Ninety-Percent Feels Too	18
The Out-Of-Office Auto Reply	105
The Pacific Railroad Ties	42
The Paradox Of Reading	54
The Parapets Of You	106
The Passage I Always Need To Underline	99
The Pebble On The Edge Of The Tide	96
The Pebbles In My Pockets	8
The Petals Of Lost Books	104
The Petition	86
The Photosynthesis Of People	97
The Pinholes In My Lampshade	110
The Place Where Solitude is Born	4
The Pop Quiz	59
The Prescription	69
The Promise "Someday" Cannot Break	20
The Raw And Unapologetic	74
The Reason	109
The Reflections Lie	10
The Remnants Of Sunset	20
The Repurposed Anchors	35
The Resistance	31
The Resisting Is Like Chemo Sometimes	6
The Rest Of Tomorrow	84
The Ribcage's Secrets	65
The River Rafts	36
The Same Bird	25
The Screams Lessen	67
The Security Blanket	89

Index

The Shadow Isn't Stronger	91
The Shadows Have A Voice	7
The Sidewalk Strangers Are My Philharmonic	98
The Silence	41
The Silence Forgot You	125
The Silence Of Music	76
The Sirens Have A Home	45
The Sliding Door Won't Open With A Push	80
The Smoke In My Head (That Keeps Me From Seeing)	123
The Snowflake Mold Broke Today	11
The Sondering	50
The Soul's Front Is Not All Quiet	116
The Sound Of Breathing Played Backwards	124
The Sound The Tree Made When It Fell In The Middle Of The Woods	18
The Space Around The Stars	110
The Space Between The Lines	118
The Spoon Wrapped Around My Index Finger Is The Reason I Can Write Today	40
The Stars Are Your Headlights	36
The Storm's Eye Is A Mirror	111
The Stranger Tides	15
The Streets Are Filled With Better Things Than Regret	54
The Stroller's Red Umbrella	21
The Struggle Of Sunset	4
The Subtext	7
The Sunburn	75
The Sunrises You Sleep Through	16
The Tears On Fifth Street	65
The Test Said I Wasn't An Empathizer	24
The Texture Of Plane Windows	110
The Texture Of Snow Melt	56
The Thank You Note	43

hello, dear one...

The Theses Of My Veins	73
The Things It's Okay To Say Today	23
The Things That Do Not Matter	112
The Things Yesterday's "Someday" Missed	38
The Three-Year-Old Can't Fall Asleep Yet	22
The Time I Caught Myself Dreaming	88
The Tree Outside Of The Forest Is My Favorite	114
The Tree Swings	16
The True Gift Of Friendship	52
The Truest Birthday Gift	119
The Truth About Idioms	19
The Turn I'm Glad You Took	55
The Unkempt Souls	5
The Unseen Tree Still Falls	92
The Unselfishness Of Candlelight	120
The Unwritten Rule	82
The Value Of Nursery Rhymes	78
The Waking-Up Is The Hardest	46
The Walkway Doesn't End Here	9
The Waves That Try To Trap Us	71
The Way Bitterness Takes Hold	88
The White Fire Needs The Black	66
The Windshield Wipers Ruin The Metaphor	44
The Word To The Wise	113
The World Is A Bully Sometimes	21
The World Is Our Noise- Canceling Headphones	22
The Wrong Side Of The Bus	48

FOR YOU

hello, dear one...

For you

These pages are for your journey, dear one. Your words matter too.

hello, dear one...

For you

hello, dear one...

For you

hello, dear one...

Made in the USA
Charleston, SC
02 February 2016